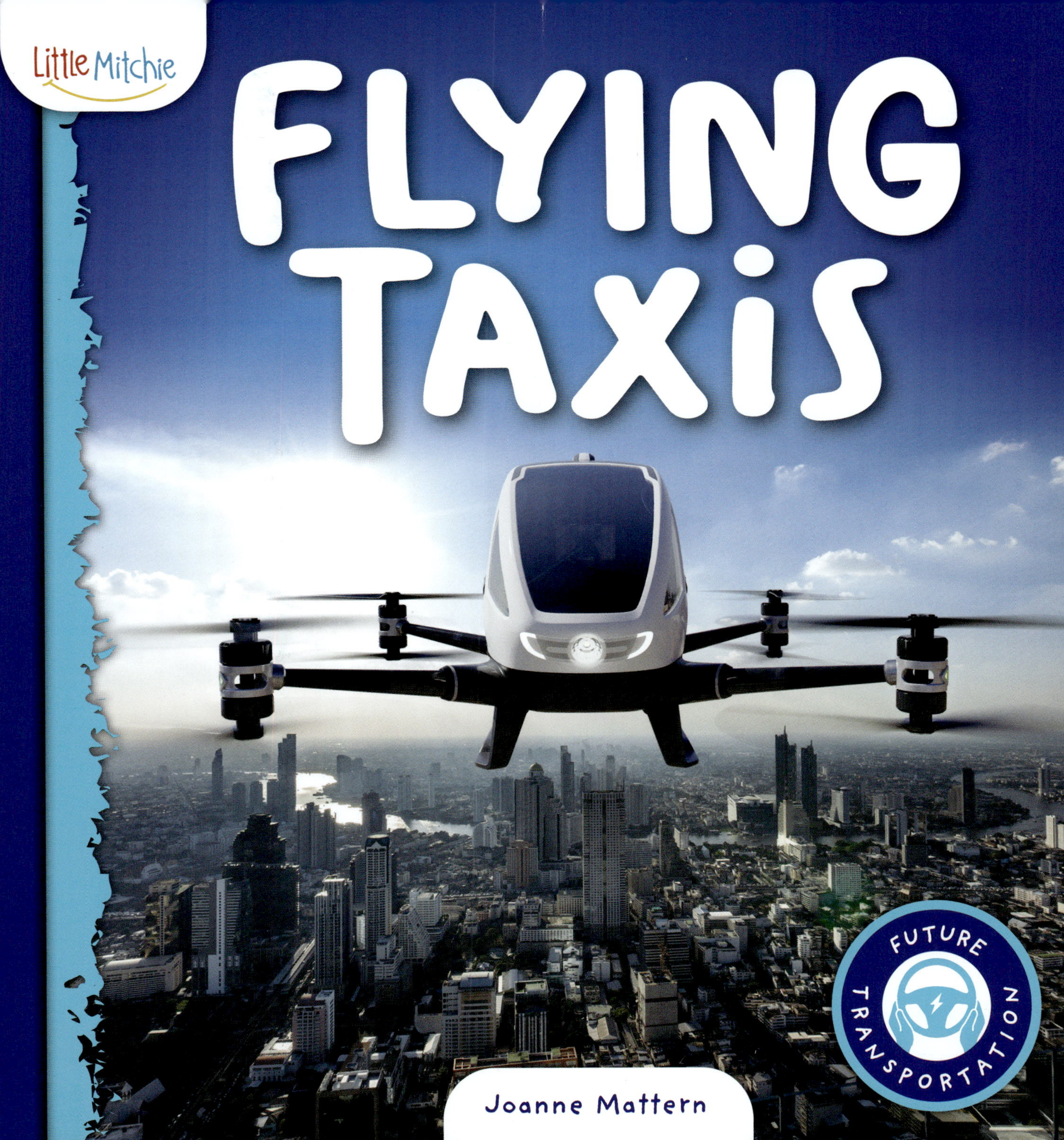
Little Mitchie
FLYING TAXIS
FUTURE TRANSPORTATION
Joanne Mattern

CREATING YOUNG NONFICTION READERS

Little Mitchie books spark curiosity and support early nonfiction reading for students in Grades 2-3. Designed to build vocabulary, support second language learners, and prepare readers for middle-grade content, each book includes helpful tips for parents and educators to build confidence and deepen understanding of the world.

TIPS FOR READING NONFICTION WITH BEGINNING READERS

Talk about Nonfiction

Begin by explaining that nonfiction books give us information that is true. The book will be organized around a specific topic or idea, and we may learn new facts through reading.

Look at the Parts

Most nonfiction books have helpful features. Our *Little Mitchie* titles include color photographs and graphic aids, a table of contents, a glossary, and an index. Share the purpose of these features with your reader.

Color Photos and Graphic Aids

A lot of information can be found by "reading" photos, charts, maps, and other graphic aids found within nonfiction texts. Help your reader learn more about the different ways information can be displayed.

Table of Contents

Located at the front of the book, this list shows the big ideas within the text and the page numbers where they can be found.

Glossary

Located at the back of the book, the glossary defines key words and phrases that are related to the topic. These words and phrases can be found in the text in colored type.

Index

Located at the back of the book, an index is an alphabetical list of topics and the page numbers where they can be found.

With a little help and guidance about reading nonfiction, you can feel good about introducing a young reader to the world of *Little Mitchie* nonfiction books.

Little Mitchie is an imprint of:

Mitchell Lane
PUBLISHERS

2001 SW 31st Avenue
Hallandale, FL 33009
mitchelllanepub.com

First Edition, 2027.

Author: Joanne Mattern
Designer: Bobbie Houser
Editor: Tricia Hoffman

Library of Congress Cataloging-in-Publication Data
Title: Flying Taxis / by Joanne Mattern

Description: Hallandale, FL :
Mitchell Lane Publishers, [2027]

Identifiers:
ISBN 979-8-89260-867-1 (library bound)
ISBN 979-8-89260-964-7 (eBook)

Library of Congress Control Number: 2026936105

PHOTO CREDITS
Alamy: RichardBaker, 13; Xinhua, 19; ZUMA Press, Inc., 20; Dreamstime: Lobach19792006, 14; Mmantas582, 21; Shutterstock: Kinwunz, cover, 1, 5; Alexander Steamaze, 7; Kinwunz, 9; Chesky, 11; Tarek ibrahim, 12; Rick Siu, 17; Tatiana Shepeleva, 22.

TABLE OF CONTENTS

Chapter One

UP AND AWAY!

George was excited to fly over the city. “Are we taking a helicopter?” he asked.

“No,” his father said. “We are taking a flying taxi.”

George was puzzled. He’d seen taxis driving in the city streets. How could a taxi fly?

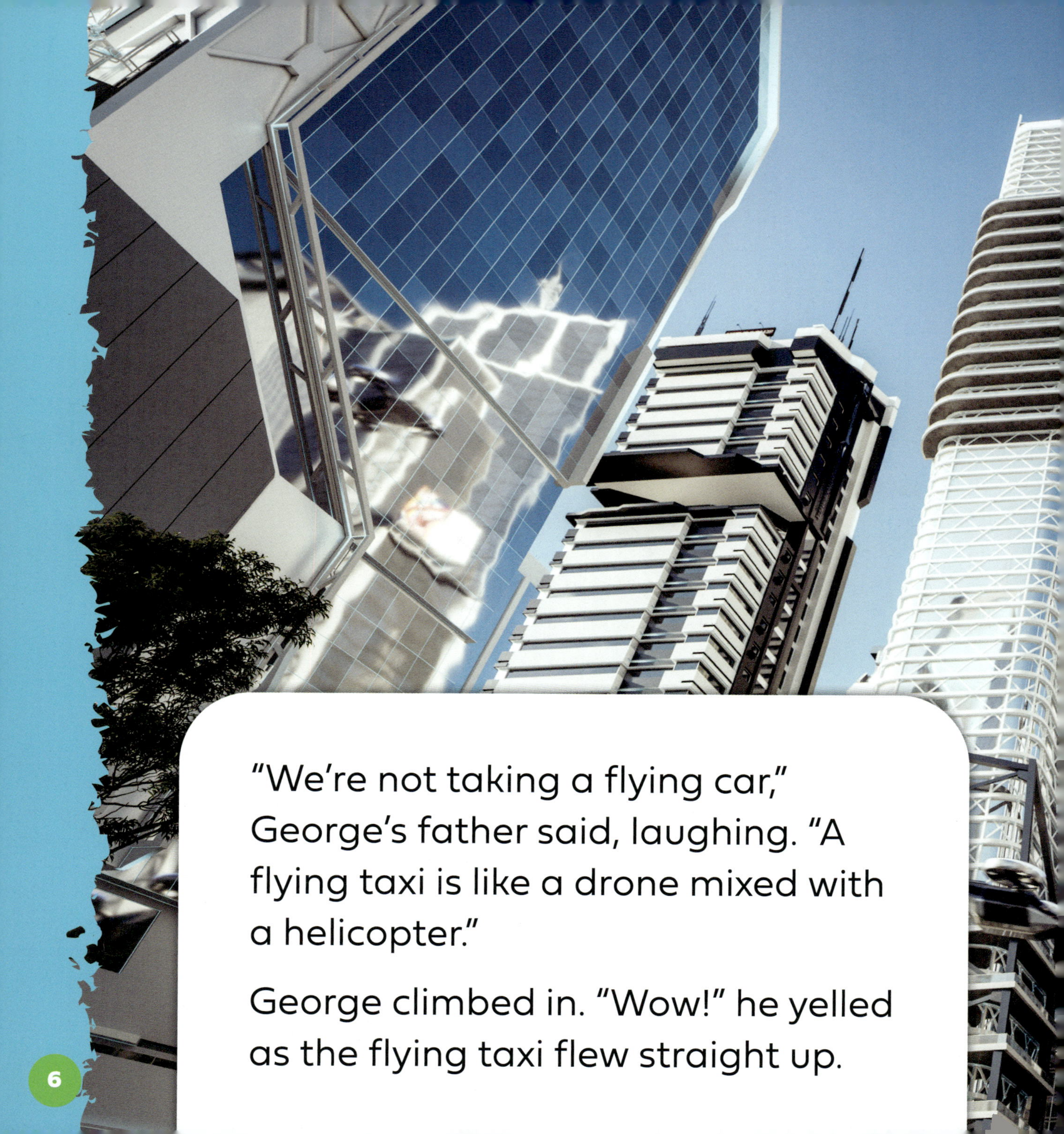

"We're not taking a flying car," George's father said, laughing. "A flying taxi is like a drone mixed with a helicopter."

George climbed in. "Wow!" he yelled as the flying taxi flew straight up.

The flying taxi zipped through the air. It felt like being in an airplane.

"That was great!" George said when the **craft** touched down 10 minutes later. "I can't wait to fly in a taxi again."

QUICK FLIGHT

Some flying taxis can fly as fast as 200 miles (322 kilometers) per hour!

Chapter Two

Flying Taxis Today

Flying taxis are called eVTOLs (ee-vee-tolz). That stands for electric **vertical** takeoff and landing aircraft. They look like helicopters, but eVTOLs are different.

TAKING CHARGE

Like electric cars, an eVTOL needs to be charged up before it flies. An eVTOL can travel just 100 to 150 miles (161 to 241 kilometers) on a single charge.

A helicopter uses a big gas-powered motor that moves one large **rotor**. A flying taxi uses several small electric rotors that are battery powered.

Helicopters have been around for nearly 100 years, but flying taxis are new. In 2023, a Chinese company received the first **official** document saying its eVTOL was ready to fly.

A TIGHT FIT
A flying taxi can only hold two to eight people.

eVTOLs are quieter than planes and helicopters. They also produce less **pollution** and are easier to fly.

Today, people take taxis on short trips through a city. eVTOLs would be used the same way. Flying is much faster than driving through crowded streets!

Chapter Three

FUTURE FLYING

You can't take a flying taxi just yet, but that will probably change soon.

More than 150 companies are building eVTOLs. These taxis can fly straight up and down, **hover**, and **tilt** to move through tight spaces.

LOOK UP, NEW YORK!

In 2023, a company called Joby flew an eVTOL over New York City.

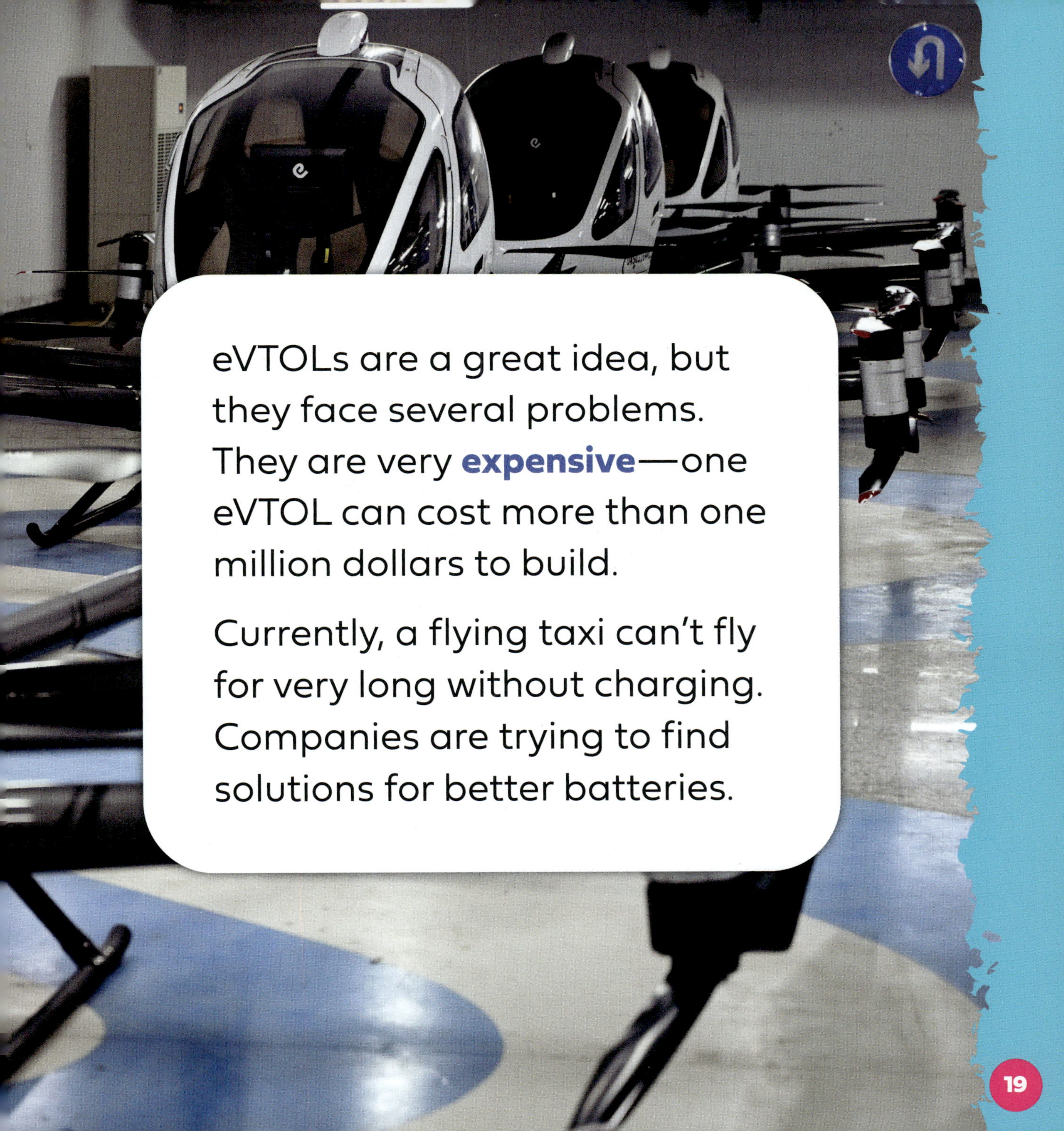

eVTOLs are a great idea, but they face several problems. They are very **expensive**—one eVTOL can cost more than one million dollars to build.

Currently, a flying taxi can't fly for very long without charging. Companies are trying to find solutions for better batteries.

Safety is important. Companies have to prove their flying taxis are safe for passengers.

People are working to solve these problems. Some experts say we could see eVTOLs in the sky by 2030.

LET'S LOOK AT A FLYING TAXI

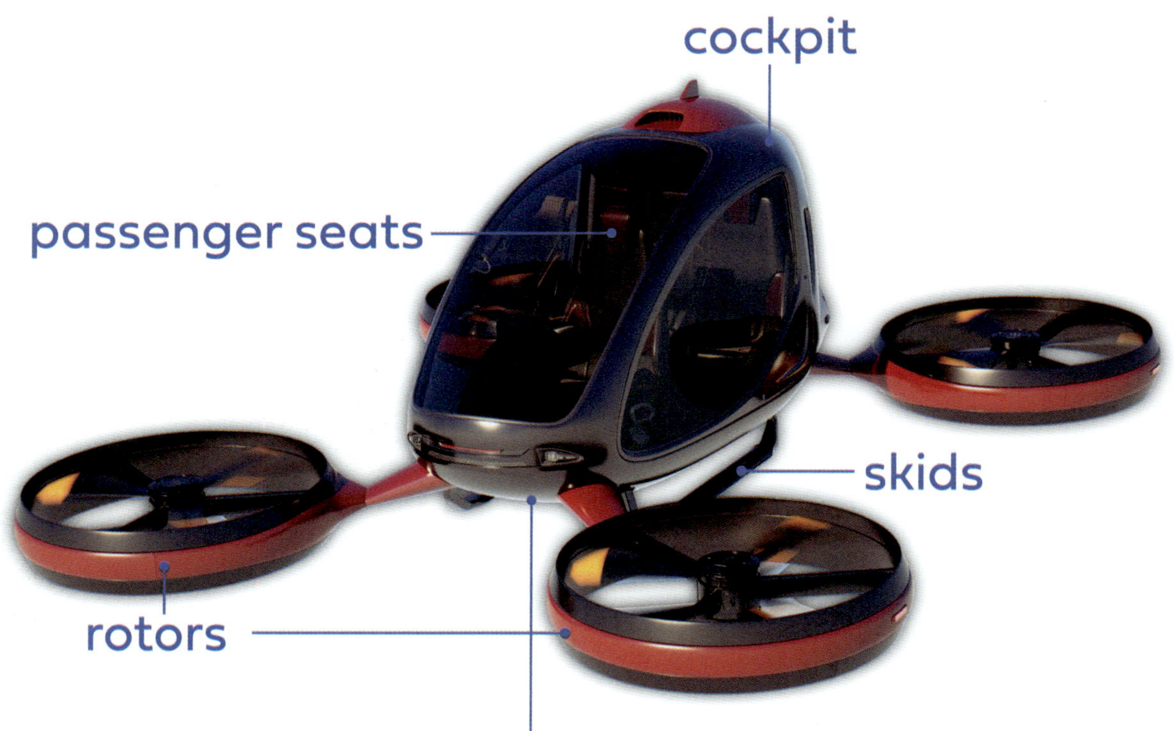

GLOSSARY

craft (kraft) a vehicle for traveling through the air

expensive (ik-spen-siv) costing a lot of money

hover (huhv-ur) to remain in one place in the air

official (uh-fish-uhl) having authority

pollution (puh-loo-shuhn) harmful materials that damage the air, water, and soil

rotor (roh-tur) the part of an engine that turns or rotates

tilt (tilt) to lean or tip to one side

vertical (vur-ti-kuhl) straight up and down

FURTHER READING

Duling, Kaitlyn. *Helicopters.* Bellwether Media, 2023.

Rathburn, Betsy. *Drones.* Bellwether Media, 2020.

ON THE INTERNET

eVTOL: Vertical Takeoff and Landing. What Does it Mean?
www.funkidslive.com/learn/amys-aviation/vtol-vertical-take-off-and-landing-what-does-it-mean/
Amy's Aviation explains the different kinds of eVTOLs and how they work.

Helicopter
https://kids.britannica.com/students/article/helicopter/274829
Learn how helicopters fly and how they are used in this Britannica Kids encyclopedia entry.

INDEX